# Rabbi Brian's Reluctant Revelation

Rabbi Brian Zachary Mayer

I didn't get the calling until I dropped out of being a real rabbi. I'd always assumed people who talked about a personal calling from the divine were nutter butters.

And, I'm not a nutter butter.

I'm one of the most rational, analytical people I know. I was captain of the math team in high school. I went to rabbinical school intent on parsing the ancient Hebrew religion into postulates, axioms, and theorems.

And, then, when Judaism and the G-O-D word proved to be straw horses, I thought I would have a full life in which I would occasionally field the question, So, you used to think you wanted to be a rabbi?

But, that's not what happened.

---

---

It all begins at Mount Sinai. I'm born there. Mount Sinai hospital, Manhattan, NYC, January 8, 1970.

Eight days later there is supposed to be a bris—a ritual circumcision. Why on the eighth day? Tradition.

So, on the eighth day after my birth—nothing special happens. I'd already been circumcised in the hospital.

My parents aren't orthodox. They are hip, avant-garde – unorthodox.

They do go to shul on Rosh Hashanah and during their fast on Yom Kippur. Passover seders are cherished family times.

Then again, every December 25th there is gift-giving. It's not Christmas, mind you. "We're Americans," my mom says, "and it's a national holiday."

At thirteen I become a man by memorizing the English phonetics of Hebrew and pretend to read from the Torah. To celebrate this achievement, there is a party with a magician, a robot, and thirteen different food stations.

As a kid, I know I'm Jewish. While attending a Dutch Reformed Church school, I don't sing the parts of Christmas carols that mention Jesus by name. I know it's wrong.

So is having a glass of milk with a steak. On the other hand, sushi is fair game. So is Prosciutto di Parma, probably because of its continental connotation and Grandma not knowing it is really ham.

---

Passover week 1985. A Friday night as the sun is going down. Our family of four is in the black Volvo station wagon with tan leather interior, heading to beautiful Litchfield County, Connecticut, our place in the country.

We are discussing dinner. My older sister Sari and I discover a coupon for Burger King that will expire on Sunday.

So, we take a family vote and go to a Burger King drive-thru. We take the buns off bacon-double cheeseburgers and substitute matzah. American Judaism at its finest.

---

---

I choose to go to college at Tufts, just outside Boston, because I can get home in a jiffy for holidays and family celebration—and because the catalog touts courses in pre-architecture. I figure architecture, my chosen profession since before I can spell the word, will bridge my loves of creativity and mathematics. Plus, mom thinks I'll be good at it.

Freshmen year, I cross College Avenue to attend a Chanukah latke-making party at the Hillel office. In the dingy, second-floor kitchen of what used to be the Medford Fire Station, I join the shredded-potato-frying assembly line. I feel a connection with these people.

Pretty soon, after engineering classes in the building next door, I make it a habit of visiting the Hillel's library of books and audio cassettes. I thumb through The First Jewish Catalog and The Jewish Book of Why.

• How does "Don't boil a kid in its mother's milk" mean no milk and meat together?

• Who said chicken and milk is taboo?

• How was it calculated that one must wait six hours after having meat before enjoying an ice cream?

For the questions for which I can't find answers. I buttonhole the affable Rabbi Jeff Summit, Hillel's executive director. "Could one have a kosher cheese-burger if the cheese were dairy free?"

After many such questions, he tells me I'll one day ask him for a recommendation in applying for rabbinical school. I laugh out loud.

But I do have this inexplicable and compelling desire to learn more about what it means to be a Jew. And, I figure, no way better than to study to become a rabbi.

My decision shocks my parents. "What kind of job is that for a nice Jewish boy?" dad says.

Mom coerces me to go for aptitude testing. The results show a talent for visualizing three-dimensional space, which, she highlights, pointing right at architecture.

Still, my mind is made up, though I know I'm disappointing my mom.

The year after graduation from Tufts, I apologize to Rabbi Summit and ask him for a recommendation.

---

---

Spring of 1993. Cincinnati, Ohio.
My dad drops me off for the start
of my two-day rabbinical school
interview. The century-old Hebrew
Union College building, in the
Richardsonian Romanesque-style,
looks like a castle. I wonder how
many times after tomorrow I will
be going through those doors.

Can I really see myself as a rabbi?
What the heck am I doing here?

I'm early. Very early. Very nervous.

I take a walk along tree-lined Clifton Avenue, listening to a favorite mix-tape. Don't worry be happy.

"Good Morning," I hear someone say.

I'm startled and don't respond. I'm a New Yorker. My first time being greeted on the street by a stranger.

---

---

The interview process begins with psychological tests. Minnesota Multiphasic Personality Inventory (MMPI) – 567 true-or-false questions. I'd heard if you answer true about enjoying arranging flowers you're branded gay and the school won't admit you. There are a few questions about flowers. I laugh aloud.

And, after the psychologist shows me a bunch of inkblots, I lean in and say, "Listen, doc, I know I'm supposed to say I see vaginas here, but I just don't. They all look like butterflies."

Dad picks me up in the 19-foot RV we'd driven from New York. When we arrive at the campground he jokes, "Where's the Jewish section?"

"Wherever we park," I say.

We make pork chops on the barbecue. Seems appropriate. At the ordination of its first graduates as rabbis in 1883, the leaders of liberal Judaism here hosted an elegant, sumptuous nine-course non-kosher banquet.

Liberal Judaism has always been unrelenting in its radical cry of personal autonomy.

---

---

Day two of the interview process. I wait in a small foyer until a committee will test me to see whether I have the right stuff for admission.

A professor stops by, introduces himself. Tells me he is one of the few people who can identify four different Boston accents.

I really don't care.

But, I'm also suspicious. Is this a test? Rabbis have to appear interested with people blathering.

I feign interest easily enough.

But, it doesn't take my mind off the big issue I'm grappling with. How I will answer when they ask about my belief in God?

I don't know, but am certain lying about believing in God at a rabbinical school interview is the kind of thing God wouldn't take too lightly.

Professor Boston takes his leave. Moments later, the double doors open and I'm ushered into a boardroom with a giant conference table . Six professors and rabbis on one side. Me on the other.

The pleasantries end as Dr. Gary Zola, the director of admission asks, "So, Brian, tell us, why are you applying to rabbinical school."

"Dr. Zola, I'm not going to lie, I like the idea of a job that offers free wine on Friday nights."

It gets a laugh.

"But, more seriously?" he probes.

"Well, Donna Millmore, a guidance counselor at Tufts, asked me to contemplate what I would like to look back on having done in twenty-five years time. And, well, even if I had become a well-known architect, even if I had won awards, well, it just doesn't have a sense of meaning. I want to have a meaningful life, a meaningful job, and if it comes with free wine, all the better."

It's a bit enjoyable for me to be the center of their attention.

I answer questions about the Hebrew class I'm taking, about the magic camp I've attended since I was nine, about the software I was using to digitize a prayer book into a computer, about tutoring teens for the mathematics section of the SATs.

Then I'm asked, "What are your beliefs in the messiah?"

"I don't have any."

"Surely you must have some. Tell me something about your

understanding about Judaism's take on a messiah. "

"I'll make you a deal. You let me into the school, I'll learn, and report back to you in a year."

"I'm going to push you on this one, Brian. Tell us something."

"Okay, fine. I'm confused. I don't quite get the whole Messiah of David and the Messiah of Aaron thing. Does the Temple need to be standing for either or both? I don't know. Doesn't seem like either has arrived yet, but, as I said, I don't know and that's why I want to come to school and learn."

My thinking: if I got in, I would learn about Jewish tradition, my heritage, and other things I really don't know much about. And, maybe I'd find out there is a God, and serve on God's team—with a title. Or maybe I'd find out there is no God, drop out and hear from people at social gatherings, Is it true you once thought you would become a rabbi?

A week later, back home on the Upper West Side of Manhattan, I answer the white, wall-mounted push-button phone in the kitchen.

It's Dr. Zola with the news: I'm in.

"You really impressed the committee with both your IQ score and knowledge about the Messiah of Aaron. You really impressed us with that one. A few of the committee members didn't know about the supposed Moshiach from the line of Aaron and Zadok."

He didn't let on if he knew about it.

I confess, "I learned it in a course I took last semester at Columbia from a very wise nun, Dr. Celia Deutsch."

Why I can't stop myself from attempting to impress will be a later topic for therapists. "The class was called, Judaism at the time of Jesus."

"Very good."

"Dr. Zola, I have a question: Why didn't you or anyone ask me about my beliefs in God?"

"Well, this might be something your nun friend didn't know—Judaism doesn't require anyone to believe in God."

I didn't know that.

And, thank God.

---

---

Next year in Jerusalem, aka my first year of rabbinical school. Most of my classmates claim two qualities I don't have. They feel a magnetic pull to Israel and they have heard "callings."

I was never bitten by the Israel bug. To me it's a piece of land, like many others. Interesting, to be certain, but no more magical than Istanbul or New York.

Whenever asked about a calling, I say, "I think it must have gone to voicemail."

A fellow student, Dave Burstein, and I form a bond because neither of us exactly fits in. We never attended Jewish summer camps. I found my tribe at magic camp, Dave found his at Outward Bound.

We sign-up together to be the b'alei tefilla—service leaders, literally service lords—for a Saturday morning service on the Hebrew Union College campus.

Our classmates fill the front rows.
A tour-bus load of over-eager
Christian tourists is in the back
rows, voyeurs looking for Jesus in
Hebrew prayers.

The thing is, Jesus didn't speak
Hebrew.

Neither do I. Not fluently, anyway.

Dave announces: "pesukei
d'zimra."

I follow with the English
translation: "Verses of singing."

We improvise lyrics in Hebrew and English with the traditional words of a traditional opening, Psalm, 96.

"Sing"

"Unto"

"God"

"A new"

"Song."

It's awkward as we continue the service with our rapid-fire translations, even when we spice it up, reading a line from Jonathan

Livingston Seagull. "You have the freedom to be yourself, your true self, here and now, and nothing can stand in your way."

We stick with our vision. It bombs beginning to end, as we stand at the exit door, shaking hands with those exiting.

The only ones remaining are the dean of the school, Shaul; our favorite teacher, Moshe, and our tefillah (prayer) instructor, Ezri.

Shaul motions for me to close the door behind me.

A merciless critique follows.

Moshe: "There were people who came this morning who had wanted to pray and you denied them the opportunity with your theatrics."

Shaul: "What you did was appropriate for a college student. Not here."

Ezri: "Richard Bach is not a Jewish teacher."

Dave and I share the shame and the blame. We avoid each other the rest of the year.

Three months later, still in Jerusalem, it's my turn to give a Friday night d'var torah — a teaching of torah. I am supposed to expound on the section about Nadav and Avihu, the two oldest sons of Aaron, who bring an "alien fire" before God, who promptly smites them.

Standing behind the sabbath candles, I say, "We need no longer be afraid of bringing before God alien fires."

I quote a classic line from the prayer book: "Superstition shall no longer enslave the mind, nor idolatry blind the eye."

Now comes a bit of theatrics from my many years performing magic tricks.

I raise my voice dramatically, "There is no reason for us to be afraid of different paths to the holy. There is no one path. There are no alien fires."

In swift succession, I blow out one of the shabbat candles, touch the smoldering wick with a piece of flash paper, throw the resulting flame away from me in a large arc, and then point at the relit candle. (Flash paper relights a smoldering candle.)

"The fire of truth is an eternal flame," I say. "The fire of truth is never extinguished." I end, pointing to the rekindled flame.

Moshe, my favorite teacher, dashes from the room.

I wonder if he's violently ill or I did something terribly wrong again.

I hope he had to puke.

The next day I see his face. I know it's bad. He tells me he has never seen anything so disrespectful, such blatant irresponsibility, irreverence. Throwing fire on the sabbath. Blowing out the sabbath candles. Desecrating the sanctuary.

He tells me he went home and cried to his wife, telling her he no longer could teach at this liberal school if students fail to honor tradition.

I wish I had the wisdom at the time to say, Moshe, I'm not powerful. I'm a first-year student.

Instead, I went to the bathroom and threw up.

---

---

I'm on the air-conditioned second
floor of the school's Jerusalem
library. Not looking for anything,
but wandering the stacks,
escaping the heat.

The red and white art nouveau
lettering on the spine and
intriguing title of Erich Fromm's
You Shall Be As Gods calls to me.

It's the first time I read anything
about the G-O-D word that makes
logical, reasonable sense.

And, somewhat sheepishly, it dawns on me that rational, intelligent folk have made peace with the God-concept before I came along.

Fromm talks about how the character of God, as described in the Bible, evolves as the culture of the people writing about God in the Bible evolve.

How God debuts as a jealous totalitarian ruler—because that was the notion of a ruler to our most ancient ancestors. With the story of Abraham, 1800 BCE, in the time of Hammurabi, God is depicted as a constitutional monarch. By 1300 BCE and Moses, God is portrayed as incorporeal and nameless.

Evolution.

The God character changes and grows.

Fromm posits that today we do not refer to a being when we refer to God, but instead use the word as a placeholder for our highest ideals.

Thank God I found that book.

---

End of summer, 1994. A hot classroom on Hebrew Union's downtown Los Angeles campus. A dozen of us just back from our first-year of rabbinical school in Israel sit facing a rabbi in a suit. It's bootcamp for budding rabbis.

In fourteen days, we will each be deployed to Podunks around the western United States, dots on the map that each have Jews—but not enough to support a resident rabbi. They contract with the school to take fresh recruits like us to conduct services for the High Holy Days.

I will be the "rabbi" leading Rosh Hashanah and Yom Kippur services in a community center in Sierra Vista, Arizona. I'll be so nervous the days before showtime I'll clench my jaw to the point I'll have difficulty eating.

Meantime, in this hour-long class, Rabbi Rosove, who works at Temple Israel of Hollywood, asks, "How many of you know what dukhanen is? It's Yiddish for birkat hakohanim."

Mona, as though she isn't certain says, "The priestly benediction?"

She's the Hermione Granger of our group. She knows everything.

"Yes," the rabbi before us continues, "one of the most famous blessings in the Torah. In the Book of Numbers, parshat naso—the only real thing of interest in the portion."

And then enunciating clearly so we can pick up—and then hopefully emulate—his cadence, he recites:

"May Adonai bless you and protect you.

"May Adonai deal kindly and graciously with you.

"May Adonai bestow favor upon you and grant you peace.

"In Yiddish, these words Aaron and his descendants bless the community are called dukhanen— from the Yiddish word for platform, because it used to be given from someone standing on a platform. You'll give this blessing at the end of weddings, at the end of bar and bat mitzvahs, and if you choose to, at your high holiday pulpits."

Later, doing research I'll find out these words aren't originally from the Book of Numbers as we were told. They were found on silver amulets in a burial cave outside of Jerusalem before Numbers was codified.

That biblical source material exists outside the Bible makes sense. What wows me is people have been using this blessing for more than two-and-a-half millennia.

I ask, "Rebbe, how about some tips, pointers, how tos on delivering the blessing?"

"First, know while it used to be only priests, you can do this even if your last name isn't Levi or Cohen. Second, many people close their eyes when they do it. My grandfather used to say if you looked at the rabbi who was doing it, you would go blind and if you looked a second time, you would die. Which never really made sense, because if you went blind the first time…"

We laugh politely.

"Third, some rabbis put their prayer shawls over their heads when they do the blessing. I'd say this is completely optional. And fourth, there is the issue of the hands."

Mona pantomimes the Star Trek Vulcan-salute with both hands and says, "Both sets of hands, two fingers, space, two fingers, with thumbs touching."

"Yes," Rosove approves.

He leans in, toward us, as though to tell a secret.

"I don't do the Dr. Spock Vulcan thing. It's not that I can't."

He demonstrates with both hands.

"It's that Leonard Nimoy sits front and center in my congregation and I always start to laugh when I think of doing it in front of him."

I think this ancient blessing might be summarized in the four words penned by Gene Roddenberry— Live long and prosper.

---

I'm in the boondocks of Arizona, billeted with Joe and Enid and their pride of cats, a few miles from Tombstone and the OK Corral. We're having breakfast.

"Rabbi, you probably in all your education never knew here in Sierra Vista we invented something world famous," says Joe.

He calls me rabbi. It feels weird.

"I'm sorry Joe, I wasn't fully paying attention."

"You're thinking about your services and your breakfast."

"I'm thinking this is an odd job I have."

"Drive-thrus" Joe says.

"I'm sorry?"

"The first McDonald's drive-thru was created here in 1975 near Fort Huachuca because anyone in fatigues was not allowed out of their car off-post."

Not exactly valuable information for me, in this town with only a

few dozen Jews, suffering lock-jaw
anxiety, about to solo my first
Rosh Hashanah service.

But I get through it and a return
trip for Yom Kippur.

I wonder if at next year's
placement I'll wear the mitered
hat again. It felt stupid at the
Grange Hall.

---

---

There's a note in my school mailbox: Brian, Dean Bycel would like to see you immediately after classes today. I recognize the handwriting. Marci, his adorable receptionist.

"I guess when you're summoned, you summon," I say Seinfeld-like to Marci, who chuckles.

The inner-office door opens. The tall dean, in a blue blazer, says, "Come in. And thanks for coming."

"Of course, I came. I was summoned."

I sit.

"Brian, Brian," he starts, signaling exasperation.

The meeting concerns my internship and a class I'm teaching—Introduction to Judaism—at one of the two gay synagogues in L.A.

Turns out the dean heard I taught my class that Abraham, Isaac, and Jacob probably weren't grandfather, son, and grandson as presented in the Bible, that "these are just stories," that scholars agree factual recorded history starts later, around the time of King David.

"Brian, you have to be careful with whom you share the truth," the dean says.

I realize I'm living in a small Jewish fishbowl, where someone in a class complains to their rabbi that the student-teacher questions the stories in the Bible and that it's a big enough deal for the rabbi to call the dean to then castigate me.

We chat a little until it's time for me to leave.

"I thank you for taking this in good spirits, Brian. I certainly hoped you would."

"Well, I thank you for the admonition," I say, smiling, "summon me anytime."

He laughs.

"Hey," I casually say, "Might you recommend a therapist? I have some things I feel the need to work out."

I think, but do not say, Like, how I'm not supposed to teach what I know to be true.

---

---

For my twenty-fifth birthday,
January 8, 1995, I decide to
celebrate by getting stoned for
the first time. I figure it will be fun.
A laugh. A memorable escape
from the cerebral, constantly
thinking, thinking, thinking.

One of my classmates scores
some marijuana for me. Another
joins us.

Before the three of us gather in
my L.A. apartment, I bake a batch
of chocolate-chip cookies. Though

I have no experience smoking pot,
I know to plan for the munchies.

My newfound supplier fashions a
pipe from the cardboard tube of a
roll of paper towels, a piece of
tinfoil and a safety pin. We smoke.

I find myself on the tan carpet of
my living room, munching cookies
under a white woven blanket. Bull
Durham, the Kevin Costner
baseball movie, is playing on the
TV.

"When's Rocky the Squirrel going
to show up?" I ask.

Laughter.

"Isn't this Bullwinkle?" I persist.

More laughter.

"How long have I been eating this cookie?" I say. "I can't remember a time when I wasn't eating it."

For the rest of the semester, one of the witnesses refers to me as "Winkle the eternal cookie."

I forgive them. They will be instrumental in introducing me to the love of my life.

---

In the elevator of my apartment at 101 North Croft Avenue near the Beverly Center, I run into Doris, who tells me that her Stan died a few weeks ago.

She invites me to dinner.

Over a home-cooked meal of broccoli and steamed potatoes I learn that Stan was a signmaker, didn't make a lot of money, but enough for them to go on a couple of cruises.

She misses him so much it hurts.

This is part of being a rabbi. Just listening to the story of Stan's life and how Doris is now alone.

I return to my apartment, sit at the dining room table/study area, pick up a dark blue, Pentel felt-tip pen, ready to attack a legal pad.

But anger like I've never experienced surfaces. My hands are shaking.

I slam the pen into the yellow paper, crushing the point.

I start to cry. Bang the table with my fist.

How dare God be God!

How dare God take Stan and from Doris!

Fuck you!

Still sobbing, I grab another pen, a ballpoint, and begin a Dear John letter to God.

I tell God we are officially breaking up. Never mind that I never believed in an entity defined by the letters G-O-D.

I write:

I need a break.

I feel like I'm the only one in this relationship doing active and honest work.

And, if no one has ever told you, you are not a good communicator. You might want to look into that.

---

---

Late summer of 1995. My study partner is ill with mono. I coordinate friends to bring her meals. One of them is her former classmate from Brown.

We meet on Labor Day, when I bring enough food for the three of us.

Jane and I date a while. Then, I break up with her, terrified of where this is heading—commitment, marriage.

But, I tell her it's because she's not Jewish. (She was brought up Protestant and went to Catholic school.)

We still hang out. She wants to be friends.

She even makes a shabbat dinner for me one Friday night. She bows her head, says, "Dear God," and talks to God. It's not a traditional prayer, more of a monologue. I find it odd. But, I guess, so is writing God a letter.

Why am I afraid of getting involved with the woman who will one day become my wife and mother of my children?

Is her being Jewish that important to me?

Years later, I will tell my rabbinical colleague, Debbi, "I distinctly remember feeling icky taking a ride in a friend's family Chrysler," pronouncing it CHRIST-ler.

"I totally get it," she says. "It's something goyish, forbidden.

Treif. Like singing Christmas songs and saying either Jesus or Christ."

"And the first time I kissed Jane after finding out her middle name was Marie, it was weird."

"A visceral response. Happened without thought."

"Do you know about caught and taught?" I ask.

"I don't believe I do."

I explain that taught is school stuff, like times tables, knowledge. But, it's not all we know. There are also the things we just picked up, we caught. Like to turn and face the doors of the elevator. Taboos aren't taught, they're caught.

"Which is why we have visceral reactions to the image of Jesus on a cross – or Christ-lers," I add.

"Or kissing someone outside your religious group."

---

---

Thursdays after school, I drive to Brentwood, get the No. 4 at Sak's Terriaki Chicken—dark meat, rice, a cold salad with delicious dressing, and a side of fried oysters—and then walk to my therapist's office.

Dr. Victor Morton helps me deal with matters academic, vocational, and personal.

When professor Rachel Adler assigns an exegesis on a Bible passage to pull out the original meaning in the text, Victor gives me the courage to write there is no such thing—that all meaning is brought in. He helps me stand my ground and not comply with the professor's request for a rewrite.

He also helps me figure out what to do about this girl, Jane, the intoxicating, fabulous, blonde shiksa goddess whose heart I broke and still wants to be my friend.

I admit the more time I spend not dating her, the more I find I'm falling in love.

Victor tells me to take the relationship a week or two at a time, not needing to know if it will work out.

"Let's just date for two weeks and see how it goes," I suggest to Jane

We keep adding weeks. Kissing Jane Marie is no longer akin to pastrami with mayo on white bread. It's more like a perfectly warm potato knish.

My two years in L.A. are winding down. The next school year is in New York.

One evening, outside the Koo-Koo-Roo, a chicken joint on Beverly Boulevard near my apartment, I up the ante. "Let's experiment with living together next year in the Village."

---

---

Jane and I move into 184
Thompson Street in Greenwich
Village, near both our schools.
She is finishing her master's in
social work at NYU.

Hebrew Union has campuses in
Cincinnati, Jerusalem, Los
Angeles and New York. The brick-
and-glass building on West Fourth
and Broadway is across the street
from a dive Japanese restaurant. I
probably would never have
applied to the school in the first
place if the only option was living

in Cincinnati, where the main attractions are Graeter's Ice Cream and Skyline Chili.

---

---

On this day in my fourth year, I'm with twelve future rabbis in Professor Hoffman's fourth-floor classroom. Dr. Hoffman doesn't educate by filling pails—asking us to memorize and regurgitate—he lights fires.

His Muppet-infused body pantomimes his words as he asks, "Tell me, why do people close their eyes and wave their hands before their closed eyes when they light shabbat candles?"

Jonah Pesner who will become the bigshot director of a major Jewish institution, answers with the traditional: "To keep from seeing the lights that couldn't be lit after the prayer was said."

Understanding this rabbinic logic, the rest of us make affirmative sounds.

In Judaism, after saying a prayer that requires an action, one is to perform that action without delay. Say the prayer for eating matzah, immediately eat the matzah. Say the prayer for drinking wine, take a sip.

However, as soon as the candle prayer is said, it is officially shabbat and no work is to be done. So, magic loophole: lite candles, close eyes, then say prayer and open eyes. TaDa!

To let us know this isn't what he was looking for, Dr. Hoffman repeats his question.

Rochelle Robins, who will become the dean of a rabbinical school, offers, "Because closing one's eyes and making those motions helps to establish the right kavanah"—the Hebrew in-speak word for intent.

Dr. Hoffman, who at this time is looking out the window onto West Fourth—perhaps to calculate the ratio of yellow cabs to passenger cars, as I do—says nothing.

"Doc," I say, attempting to bring some levity, and hopefully an end to the riddle, say, "We give up. We fold. Why? Why do people close their eyes and wave their

hands before their closed eyes
when they light shabbat candles?"

"They do it that way," he
responds, still looking out the
window, "because they like doing
it that way."

---

---

Down the hall is the domain of our Bible teacher, Dr. David Sperling. A cabal of my classmates hate him. "Sperling loves the Bible the way a coroner loves a body— dead," they say. I think he's brilliant.

To Sperling, an exegesis attempting to attribute God's true meaning to Bible verse is a con.

He tells us there is no scholarly basis for the story Jews tell every Passover, that Moses led the

Israelites out of slavery in Egypt. He shatters any "evidence" Moses was real and the Exodus happened.

To ensure we understand, our semester grade is based on an essay debunking various theories proving the veracity of the Exodus.

In doing so, we are compelled to proclaim: I am an adult and acknowledge that the story of Moses is just a story.

That's why some classmates hate him.

--- ---

February 8, 1996. I propose to Jane by splicing myself into a scene of When Harry Met Sally. We watch the video in our apartment. She says yes.

She knows we have a dinner date with my parents uptown. She doesn't know about the surprise engagement party I've arranged, with guests flying in from California, Texas, Minnesota.

Twenty-eight dear friends and family are gathered in the apartment where I grew up on Central Park West.

"What would have happened if she'd said no," my cousin Darren asks.

"It would have been a great party for 29 people," I say.

We go to a nearby restaurant where a private room has been booked. "Brian, dear," my dad confides. "Do what you want, but see if you can get Jane to dye her hair brown, lose some weight, and never tell anyone she isn't Jewish. It will make things easier."

I don't tell him to go fuck himself. That will come years later.

My parents disapproval of my choice simmers.

Talking to Victor about all this by phone, he cleverly quotes Genesis: "That is why a man leaves his father and mother and is united to his wife, and they become one flesh."

---

---

I know it's only a matter of time before I will get a tap on the shoulder from one of the deans. I don't know how it will go down, but I know I'm in trouble. No one engaged (or married) to a non-Jew gets ordained.

I'm going to be kicked out.

How will I find the courage to tell my parents this thing they've finally become comfortable with—their son a rabbi—isn't going to happen?

And, because of a non-Jew.

I brace myself.

However, Jane pulls her own
surprise on me by enrolling in
Rabbi Sue Wasserman's
Introduction to Judaism class. I
help with the homework.

In the spring of 1997, in
Parsippany, New Jersey, Jane
emerges from the ritual bath as a
member of the tribe.

---

---

The New York campus is the only
one that allows us to pick our own
thesis topic. I propose: Pop
Culture's Conceptualizations Of
The Divine. I re-watch the movie
Oh, God! and also try to divine
the theology behind the song
What if God Were One of Us?

The associate dean, Rabbi Aaron
Panken, writes on my proposal:
Not Jewish enough. Rethink,
Resubmit.

I come back with: How pop culture's conceptualizations of the divine correlate with classic Jewish depictions of God.

Let's meet, he replies.

"I'll make you a compromise," he says. "Write about modern Israeli culture's conceptualizations of the divine — that's more Jewish."

No, it's not, I think. And why would I want to do that anyway? I don't live in Israel.

"Can I write about free will?" I ask. "How would you feel about that?"

He buys it.

I become an expert in Freedom of will: Jewish Views, 10th-15th Centuries.

I plan to find out how these long-ago Jews dealt with an omnipotent, all-knowing God, with the power to reward and punish, and, at the same time, the free will to live their lives.

I'll write it next year, three-thousand miles away.

---

---

An opportunistic Los Angeles synagogue where I'd previously interned—not wanting to compete for my services as a rabbi on the open market the following year—convinces the school to let me out early. The deal is I can finish my fifth year remotely if I return to New York to give my senior sermon to the whole school. Eighty percent rabbi means I'm paid four-fifths of a first-year rabbi's salary of $55,000.

Jane and I fly back to L.A. And, on July 1, 1997, I officially start work as the junior rabbi at Temple Judea in Tarzana, a wealthy, progressive San Fernando Valley suburb of 40,000 named for the estate of Johnny Weissmuller.

In my office, instead of putting certificates and diplomas on the wall, I arrange a message in a series of small, black, Ikea Fiskbo frames: Religion ought not shackle or limit people in their attempts to seek the divine, it should set them free.

The congregation discovers what they bargained for when I conduct High Holy Days services. Me, in a white robe, preaches the same sermon to two shifts of celebrants in the main sanctuary and to another group at an overflow service.

More than a thousand people hear the words of their new rabbi.

"Ladies and Gentlemen, dear friends I have not met, I stand here about to deliver my real rabbi first sermon to you. It will focus on imploring you to become an organ donor."

I pause and attempt to deliver the next sentence as if improvised. "I didn't know exactly what else to preach on."

Pockets of awkward laughter.

"That's not true," I say. "I knew what else I could preach on. And here, ladies and gentlemen, are the titles of the top ten high holiday sermons that you will not be hearing.

"Number ten. Shofar: Cruelty to animals or just blowing hot air?

"Number nine. A great big fish and other stories.

"Number eight. The book of life: Five-thousand-seven-hundred-and-fifty-seven years on the best seller list.

"Number seven: Fasting your way to forgiveness.

"Number six. Judaism: It's not just for the high holidays anymore.

"Number five. How to pick the lock on the gates of repentance.

"Number four. The two-outfit-four-day dilemma."

Laughter erupts.

"Number three. Is full redemption possible without a receipt?

"Number two. Rosh Hashanah: is that final 'h' really necessary?

"And, number one. Please don't get high on the high holidays."

It kills.

They thank me for making them laugh and keeping it real.

--- ---

The Little Brown Church on Coldwater Canyon Avenue in Studio City lives up to its name. I'm in the front row of the small sanctuary holding Jane's hand. In three weeks, we will fly to New York to be married. Today, late January 1998, we are gathered for a memorial service for her mom, Betty, who died in Las Vegas the previous week.

Jane squeezes my hand before she delivers her eulogy. "Mom," she says at the podium, "you wanted to be at Brian and my wedding. You asked me lots of questions. About my dress, about the music, about Jewish traditions. You loved that we worked together to silk-paint what you always referred to as the chalupa, that wedding canopy. Mom, I know when I stand under the chuppah with Brian that you will be there too."

Leading the service is a Disciples of Christ minister, Dr. Larry Keene,

who looks like a gray-haired Carl
Reiner. Though he never met
Betty, he hits all the right notes.
He makes us feel cared for. I want
to know his tricks.

Not long after, I call Larry and
invite him for breakfast.

We meet at Nat's Early Bite on the
corner of Hazeltine and Burbank.
He looks waiters in the eye and is
Boy Scout polite. We talk Bible.
And, while he is more than thirty
years my elder, we find
camaraderie in our desire to push
religion to its boundaries, to be

more inclusive, to be more honest.

We laugh comparing our different upbringings. His in the rural Pacific Northwest, setting up smudge pots for farmers, and mine riding the subway to private school in Manhattan.

"So, Larry, what do you think is the key to hitting the right notes at a funeral?" I ask.

"Depends on the circumstance, I guess. But, mainly, it's about letting the mourners know they have every right to mourn. And, to let them know love continues past our goodbyes."

I decide I want to be as kind as he is one day. Or attempt it. Over the years, he will help.

--- ---

The doors open on Jane, veiled in white. Her proud, gentile, yarmulke-wearing father, Phil, at her side.

We are on the top floor of the seven-story landmark Puck Building in SoHo, NYC.

Jane and I chose the room, in part, because it was the location of the wedding scene in When Harry Met Sally.

Jane will forever tease me that I selected the date, the day after Valentine's Day, so I could always buy anniversary flowers on sale.

The wedding is tailored by us, for us, starting with a makeover of the traditional Jewish ceremony. My boss, Rabbi Don Goor, who flew in to officiate, carries out the plans we designed back in his office in Tarzana.

It begins with Jane and me under the chuppah (marriage canopy). But, instead of the bride circling the groom seven times, Jane circles me three times, I circle her three times, and we make a seventh circle together.

Don loosely translates the Hebrew, sprinkling in the word "fabulous," and notes the fourth pole of the chuppah is held in place by a flag-stand instead of a guest, as a symbol of Betty supporting us.

We invite seven couples we admire to, in turn, join us under the chuppah and offer a blessing on qualities Jane and I hope to exemplify in our union. Hiawatha Johnson, Jr., my mentor at magic camp, wearing a black and white dashiki, gives a blessing for creativity and endless artistry. Brings me to weep.

The ceremony ends with each of us—not just the groom—breaking a glass.

A traditional Jewish reception follows.

We dance the night away.

And rub Ben Gay into each
other's feet before going to bed.

---

---

Jane and I are living in a two-bedroom house we buy in Van Nuys, about a fifteen-minute drive from Temple Judea in my forest-green Christ-ler Sebring convertible. Jane is interning as a psychotherapist at a medical center on Sunset Boulevard. We fly back to New York for my senior sermon.

A nice crowd of classmates, faculty and family is in the 245-seat Minnie Petrie Synagogue, Hebrew Union's modern chapel, with Yaacov Agam's acclaimed stained glass windows.

"Most all of us are familiar with the story of the whistling shepherd," I begin. I pause. I'm still cutting my teeth as an orator, refining performance techniques. I look down at my notes. Look up with my eyes only. Slowly raise my head. Lock in on the audience.

Only then do I tell the story.

"A rabbi overhears a shepherd whistling then saying to God, 'God, I love you. I love you so much that I would care for your sheep for free.' The rabbi approaches, and says, 'My dear shepherd, allow me to help. I love God so much and want to teach you the proper blessings and let me do it for you for free.'

"They study until they are satisfied knowledge has been transferred. The shepherd stops whistling and instead says the right blessings at the right time: Praise God who remembers when seeing a rainbow. Praise God who creates the vine fruits before drinking wine. Praise God who brings forth bread from the earth before eating bread."

I pick up a glass of water. Take a slow sip. Drama builds.

"But, the shepherd didn't remember which prayer was for what. Embarrassed, he never said the prayers or whistled to God again."

I pause, then deliver slowly, "the citizens of heaven, the story goes, wept, for they lost that most beautiful, pure prayer, his beautiful whistle."

Before I hit the heart of my sermon, I address the audience with a salutation I will use on this day and many more to come.

"My friends," I say, "we have gotten our path and the goal confused. We are prioritizing Judaism, not the whistle. We count how many people in the service bend their knees and stand on their toes at the proper, prescribed time, and what percentage pray in Hebrew. But, being Jewish isn't supposed to be the goal. It's supposed to be the path. The goal is to connect people with a sense of freedom. To help them to live in wonder. To connect them to the divine, however it makes sense to them."

After my sermon, it's time for one last academic critique. Scott Aaron, a trial lawyer turned rabbinical student, stands and asks, "So, how do we help people to find holiness without Judaism providing the map?"

"I don't know, Scott, but I'm willing to try to find out."

---

---

Thirty of us are congregated in the basement of Temple Emanu-El on Fifth Avenue in New York, a grand monument to wealth and progressive Judaism.

We are all wearing our tallises (prayer shawls) over the black robes reserved for formal liturgical occasions, waiting to be ordained as rabbis.

Of course, I've been working as a rabbi in Tarzana for ten months. I show my classmates my business card emblazoned: Intern Rabbi.

Eventually, we are ushered upstairs and into the front row of the enormous sanctuary.

I can't believe I didn't drop out back in Jerusalem, that I made it all the way here, I think.

On this hot day in May, the joint is nearly packed. Toddlers are running up and down the aisles.

We are being called up to the bima (dais) in alphabetical order, by both our English and Hebrew names.

I check the program. Do the math. Twenty names ahead of mine.

Each receives a sheepskin and a parting lecture from the head of the school, Rabbi Sheldon Zimmerman, out of earshot of the rest of us.

What is he talking about? Why is this taking so long? Will they ever get to my name?

Finally, I hear: "Brian Zachary Mayer, Amram Arieh-Lieb ben Naftali v'Hafkah."

Rabbi Zimmerman greets me in front of the stunning, ornate Torah scrolls in the holy ark.

He puts his hands on my shoulders and tells me I am connected directly in a line to God's revelation to Moses on Mount Sinai ... from Moses to Joshua ... from Joshua to the Elders ... from the Elders to the Prophets ... from the Prophets to the rabbis of the Great Assembly

… to Sheldon Zimmerman … to me.

Does this mean I'll now get a rabbi's full salary?

--- ---

A revelation strikes me in a sushi restaurant on Ventura Boulevard just east of Balboa. I've seen depictions of revelations in pop culture. Mine is nothing like that.

So, I'm not certain what it is when it happens. Nothing is out of the ordinary. Except there is a thought in my head that hadn't been there before and I don't know how it got there.

It happens while Jane and I are on an after-work dinner date, after she attempts to pass the ginger with her chopsticks.

"In Japan, no one passes food with chopsticks," I scold. "It has to do with a funeral rite, and in sushi dining it's considered rude."

Then, I notice clumps of wasabi in her soy sauce. Pretentious Manhattanite me realizes my bride—born in West Virginia, raised in Buffalo—doesn't know non-homogenized sauces are for sashimi, not sushi.

I'm about to instruct her how to mix in the wasabi, but the words don't come. Instead, I look at her and her adorable Rachel-from-Friends haircut. And I see her. Exactly as she is. Not as someone who needs to be saved or taught. But as the love of my life. Perfect as she is—to hell with the lumpy wasabi.

Stop the judgments, I tell myself.

I resolve to not shame Jane. Or anyone else. The world needs more love. And, as best as I can, I will do my part.

---

---

Palm Springs Hilton, a few days after Y2K doesn't end the world. The Pacific Area Reform Rabbis (PARR) assemble for our annual convention.

After dinner in the large banquet hall, we, as a kahal (community) bench (pray), with sporadic banging on tables for an exuberant birkat hamazon (grace after meal). Rabbis like to go full frum (super Jewish) when gathered as a group.

It's nice. I feel a sense of belonging. It doesn't last long.

I'm the only one who knows what's coming next. It's showtime.

I stand on my chair at the banquet table, directly under an overhead light. "Ladies and Gentlemen, if I might have your attention, please. Ladies and gentlemen … Ladies and gentlemen … " Someone dings a water glass.

Three-hundred eyes look at me, this kid rabbi. I lift a small metal

box that I hid under a napkin
throughout dinner.

In an infomercial-announcer voice
I intone: "Ladies and Gentlemen,
introducing God-in-a-Box." I hold
up the box. "Because if God is
everywhere, God must also be in
this box."

I gesture toward the left side of
the hall, making eye contact with
my old L.A. dean, "Rabbi Lee
Bycel. Do you want heavenly
desserts? Get God-in-a-Box and
put it in your kitchen and your
recipes will be divine."

I sweep my arm to the right, "Do you want better sleep? Put God-in-a-Box next to your bed and you'll be assured heavenly sleep."

Facing center. "Are you looking to have God on your side in your next argument? Bring God-in-a-Box with you wherever you go."

I conclude, "God in a box is manufactured under strict rabbinic supervision. Each and every God-in-a-Box is guaranteed to contain God."

I get off the chair. A few people deign to applaud politely.

Later that night, undaunted, I post a flyer around the hotel. It reads:

REMEMBER DAYS OF STAYING UP ALL NIGHT TALKING ABOUT GOD AND OTHER STUFF WITH FRIENDS? JOIN ME AND FRIENDS TONIGHT, MAIN LOBBY, 11PM.

I sit and wait. Colleagues walk by. A few stop to ask how it's going. I point to an empty seat next to me and pat it. They tell me they may be back later.

I wait about twenty minutes before heading to my room.

--- ---

As a rabbi at Temple Judea, I feel like a silver kiddush cup with a hole leaking wine. There are good moments that fill me up, but there is still the leak.

My cup is full when I tell a girl approaching her bat mitzvah that coming of age means she has authority over her religious life, and stand by her when she decides she doesn't want to go through with the ceremony.

My cup is full when a big crowd shows up for my adult education course called: God is dead and I don't feel too good myself: A guide to atheism within Judaism.

My cup is full when I'm true to myself at the pulpit, asking: "By a show of hands, how many of you believe in life after death?

Hands go up.

"And how many of you don't believe in life after death?"

Another show of hands.

"Finally, how many of you don't really know or just didn't raise your hands?"

Similar response.

I announce, "About a third of you believe in life after death, a third of you don't, and a third of you don't know"

I pause. "May I ask you a favor then? Would stop getting on my case when I don't answer when you ask, 'Rabbi, can you tell me, Do Jews believe in life after death?' It's complicated. It's always complicated."

By late June 2000, six months after my thirtieth birthday, the hole in my kiddush cup is letting out more than is going in. I feel my soul atrophying.

I dislike working on the day I'm supposed tell people not to work. I dislike being a humanist in a particularist's job. I just don't believe in the product enough. I don't want a paycheck from an organization that implies I believe God takes sides in favor of one religion over another. I don't want to be Judaism's pitchman

So, I tell my bosses I'm quitting.

I first tell the senior rabbi, Don Goor, a good man who flew six-thousand miles in 48 hours to conduct my wedding. He says it's a loss for the congregation but he wants me to pursue my happiness.

I tell the board of directors, who arrange a special pizza and beer farewell shabbat in my honor.

And, I tell the congregation in a newsletter: I can't preach follow your own soul if I don't follow mine.

---

---

Late summer, a year after 9/11.
I've just about abandoned the
business of pimping out Judaism.
It's a year before I will officially
take religion all the way outside
the box.

Jane has her psychotherapy
practice up and running and I take
a $3,000 gig as a rent-a-rabbi for
the High-Holy-Days.

I plan to play it straight for the
Jewish community of Solvang,
California (pop: 5,909) and anyone

within driving distance who scored an invitation for services in a conference room at the Royal Scandinavian Hotel.

I breeze through Rosh Hashanah. But then, as the Day of Atonement approaches, a new Yom Kippur sermon bubbles up within me—what I will later refer to as: My farewell to the Jews.

I stand at the podium in my white robe and Chuck Taylors. (Wearing white and no leather are Yom Kippur traditions.)

"Ladies and Gentlemen," I begin. "Friends here in Solvang. All of you have agreed to meet as members of this particular tribe on this particular evening. You people showered and made a conscious decision as to what clothing to wear."

A chuckle or two. I quickly continue, "Tonight is said to be the holiest day of the year. Tonight is said to be the anniversary of the day on which the High Priest would, after elaborate preparations, enter the Holy of Holies. To be face to face with God—which is quite amazing considering our tradition teaches none shall see God's face and live. But that's beside the point."

I pause. "And yes, when I hear the phrase holy of holies, I too think of Led Zeppelin's Houses of the Holy."

Their laughter lets me know they're with me.

"You have hired me, a ringer, an outside man, a professional, to preach to you something about atonement, something about forgiveness, something about God's role in your lives, however you understand the word God."

Long pause. "Here we are—Kol Nidrei night."

Longer pause. "I am tasked with telling you truth. And here it is: Please don't believe me."

I let the words sit in the air for a moment.

"If you are going to believe me, a religious professional, when I say one thing, let it be this: Do not listen to me."

---

I go to the Church of the Valley, not far from my house in Van Nuys, where my ecclesiastical soul mate Larry Keene, the Disciples of Christ minister, has an office. I'd learned he's being forced to retire "He's not taking it well," his son-in-law told me. "He could use a friend."

The receptionist at the church's administration building says Larry is in his study. I didn't know he had a study.

I follow her directions past the baptistery, up two flights of narrow stairs, down a hall, to the door of an old storeroom.

I knock lightly and enter.

Larry is sitting in a yellow, crushed-velvet club chair. He gestures toward its twin.

"Mind yourself," he says, "the chair is lower than you might think."

As I sit, the bottles of beer I've brought in my backpack clatter. "I didn't know what type of beer you like, so I brought a few kinds."

"I've never had a taste for beer. But, thank you."

I unzip a side pocket and pull out a pint bottle of scotch.
"Whiskey?"

"No, thank you, Brian. I appreciate your thoughtfulness."

We sit in silence for a moment.

He says, "I don't know what you know, but I sure could use a friend. I am glad you are here."

He tells me what's happening. "A conservative faction within the church, having acquired positions of leadership—which I had kept them from for years—have conspired to push me out. They want something different than what I can offer."

I take a shot at a joke. "Any chance they'd be interested in a rabbi with great references who just became a free-agent?"

He laughs. "No, my friend. They want someone who will tell them what they want to hear—heaven is a real place, the Bible is a guidebook for contemporary life, Jesus is the only path to salvation. I don't think you'd fit that bill for any of that."

Larry talks out his anguish. I crack open a Sam Adams and listen.

Over the next months and years, over many meals at Mexican restaurants—his favorite—we talk about religion and the human condition.

"I don't take the Bible literally, I take it seriously," he says. "A story, even one that is not true, can be filled with truth." "There's nothing wrong with a fourth-grade understanding of the Bible—so long as you are in the fourth grade."

We talk a lot about modern New Testament scholars who urge reading the gospels with Jewish eyes. I get it. If Jesus was Jewish and the authors of the gospels were Jewish, then the whole Jesus story is a Jewish story and should be read as such.

Spirited discussions with Larry often end with him teasing, "I'd agree with you, but then we'd both be wrong."

We become the best of friends.

However, there is one thing on which we will always disagree. He believes it's okay to spoon salsa and eat it like soup.

---

---

I'm standing on a stage, a portable riser, in Temple Judea's social hall. It's been eighteen months since my last day working here as a rabbi.

On this Tuesday night, more than a hundred people have each ponied up fifteen bucks to see the premiere of a one-man show I've created called Religion Outside The Box.

Rabbi Goor introduces me.

I open with a recounting of my childhood—from Mount Sinai in New York to eating bacon-double cheeseburgers on matzah in Connecticut.

I relate the story of God telling Jonah to go clean up Nineveh, the Sin City of the Assyrian Empire, and how Jonah, not buying it, runs away.

"I am Jonah," I say. "I am Jonah because, even without knowing it at first, I was called. I am Jonah because when I realized that I had gotten a call from God, I

retreated. I am Jonah because
when God called me I insisted
that God had contacted the
wrong person. I am Jonah
because after I got a calling, I got
scared and I didn't want to tell
anyone. I was scared that my life
would irreparably be changed if I
told people that God—and I can't
really define what it is that I mean
when I say God—spoke to me.

"After all, I had at one time
written God a Dear John letter to
tell God that I was less than
satisfied with our relationship, that
I felt as though I was the only one

willing to engage in open and honest in communication.

"How could I have gotten a calling from God? I'm the rabbi who led an adult education class titled: God Is Dead and I don't feel too good myself. I thought that telling people that you had a calling from God was tantamount to telling people that Jerry's famous deli has a good and reasonably priced pastrami sandwich.

"Me? I got a calling?

"Let me be clear here, the calling wasn't the type of calling that I would have assumed callings are like based on watching movies or reading Bible stories. No well-modulated baritone voice told me anything. It was more as though every atom of my being was letting me know what it was I was supposed to do. I can't explain it much better than that. When you've had this type of experience—like when you know that the person you are with you want to spend the rest of your life with—it's that kind of thing. And, I had gotten that type of calling.

"God—from what this rationalist and self-proclaimed heretic can understand— wants me to tell people that it does not matter what path they are on as so long as they are on a path. God does not discriminate based on religious upbringing or current affiliation. God wants me to tell you that what you did religiously as a child—that you used to attend Sunday school as a child— doesn't cut it for you now as an adult. God wants me to tell you that having a membership to a church, synagogue, or Jewish Community Center does not count. God wants me to tell you that you have to take this whole religion thing into your own hands. And that that doesn't mean being overly serious about it. God wants you to enjoy your life.

"And a side-note—I'm certain about this one—God wants me to tell you using the pronouns he or she are limiting the infinite, and that's just not cool.

"As far as I can tell, my calling is to be here right now, doing what I am doing. As far as I can tell, God, the universe, my soul – whatever you want to call it – wants me to be doing what I'm doing.

I'm supposed to be here preaching to you. I know it doesn't make a lot of sense. I'm as rational as they come but, from everything that I can tell, I'm supposed to be here right now imploring you to take a look at your life, asking you to take your life and your religious life into your own hands. This is what I'm supposed to be doing."

---

---

The audience seems to be with me all the way to the end.

The Jewish Journal reviews the show:

Religion-Outside-The-Box is in a word, revolutionary. In it Mayer weaves a bewitching combination of Borscht Belt-style humor and Eastern Philosophy, gently mocking both himself and the audience while challenging the assumption that faith is a passive thing absorbed through rote

prayer and what passes for
tradition. (Think a Jewish Ray
Romano channeled through Ram
Dass). The show takes a few
interesting twists, particularly in
skits like "God and the 50-minute
Hour" in which Mayer acts the
part of the Lord Almighty in
session with a psychotherapist
and in the more "interactive"
sections (audience participation is
a must to fully absorb Mayer's
philosophy). The audience of
about 150 people — not shabby

for a Tuesday night in the Valley
— took the 90-minute show to
heart and appeared not only to
have a great time but to have
learned something as well.

---

---

About a year later, I contact the Journal to tell them about my new ROTB show: Enlightenment: 100% Guaranteed.

"We won't cover you again," I'm told, "your stuff isn't Jewish enough."

###

Rabbi Brian invites you to visit him
@rotb.org
(and sign up for his newsletter!)

CPSIA information can be obtained
at www.ICGtesting.com
Printed in the USA
LVHW051535230422
717055LV00006B/147